WRITTEN

JUDGEMENTS

VOL.4

PROPHECIES BY

BISHOP E. BERNARD JORDAN

Dedication

*This book is
dedicated to my
daughter, Bethany
Maranatha Jordan,
who will wear the prophetic
mantle of her parents,
and carry the Word
of the Lord to her
generation.*

ISBN 0-939241-46-3

Written Judgments 4
Copyright © 1998 by Bishop E. Bernard Jordan
Published by Zoe Ministries, P.O. Box 270 Church Street Station,
New York, New York 10008

Unless otherwise indicated, all Scripture Quotations are taken from
the King James Version of The Holy Bible.

Written Judgments IV is the latest addition to the set of prophetic writings that I am commanded to place in the earth by the year 2000. The prophecies will both startle and amaze you, since many of these prophecies have already begun a measure of their manifestation before I was able to complete this book.

Some of the prophecies declare the Word of the Lord concerning issues that are quite controversial, and will force you to acknowledge the Omniscience of God in all things. Other prophecies are both sobering and exhilarating, for God has declared His will and purposes for mankind.

The term "Written Judgments" may carry an inference of the wrath of God but, although many who have stood in opposition to His plan will see the anger of His Hand, there will also be those that will see the redemptive power of that same Hand, extended in power, glory and majesty.

God is doing great things in the midst of His people, for He is God, and beside Him, there is none other.

Bishop E. Bernard Jordan
Bishop of Zoe Ministries

Special Recognition & Gratitude

Special thanks to these who joined their faith with ours to make the fourth edition of the Written Judgments series possible.

Carolyn Alexander
Sharlene Allen
Gregory & Minister Shirley Headen-Anthony
Jessica Arango
Pamela Bailey
Pastor & Mrs. Hubert Banks
Mable Barnes
Harvey Beal
Ronald & Donna Bowman
George & Belinda Bradford
Roland Brown Jr.
Issac Brown
Cora Charles
Cynthia L. Clark
Columba Gaetano
James Dance
Pastors William & Jane Darrisaw
Vera De Cicco
Cheryl Deloney
Father James & Donna Duncan
Pastors Richard & Diane Eberiga
Alan & Candy Finch
Melida Foster
Jennifer Fraser
Pastor Mildred Gonzalez

Willie Hamilton

Dr. Carolyn Harrell

Fred Harris

Rachel Heggins

Nettie Henderson

Varonica Holland

Carolyn Jackson

Pastor Dolly M. Johnson & The Passiac Christian Fellowship

Ruth Johnson

Theresa Johnson

Pastor Debra A. Jordan
        "In honor of my parents,
           Pastor Mary & Deacon Charlie Berrian"

Brenda Makhanda

Flora Martin

Minnie Martin

Pastor Charles Mellette

Raja & Patricia Murthy

Mary Ann O'Connell

Shirley Parish

Tory Pitts

Sandra Reed

Theodora Reynolds

Pastor Arleen & Roderick Roberts

Dr. Arnette Robinson

Pastor Paul & Gloria Shields

Dr. Gertrude Smith

Marsha McGhie-Steinberg

Ms. Elaine Swaby

Special Recognition & Gratitude

Prophets Antonio & Ruthie Thomas
Ministers Devon & Faye Thompson
Alfreda Turner
Cheryl S.Waldron
Pastor Lucinda Whitaker
Prophetess Connie Williams
Pastors Hirron & Linda Williams
Teresa Windham LaMarr
James & Simone Wright

Chapter 1
Opening the Seals

In this chapter...
The Heavens Shall Declare His Glory 7
The Calendar System 7
Political Changes 8
Taste and See that the Lord is Good 9
The Hour of Transition 10
The Wish of Death 12
Emerging Voices. 12
The Mystery of the Prophets. 15

The Word of the Lord came unto me saying, "You are entering into a new season that I am bringing forth in the earth. This is the season that you shall see many unusual things coming forth within your galaxy -- things that will literally amaze you."

The Heavens Shall Declare His Glory
"The seasons of the heavens declaring My glory shall intensify more and more. The days of extremity will come, and men will take a new interest and shall look deeper into space. I shall cause you to experience life in forms that you have never known, and the days of scientific discoveries will astound your imaginations in this day," saith the Lord.

The Calendar System
"The days are forthcoming that you shall see other planets entering into your galaxy. This will be the sign of the times,

and shall witness that you have entered into a new dimension. Many will marvel and ponder, "What kind of days are we heading for now?"

Political Changes

"The days will come that there shall be changes in the calendar system that now exists. This will be the season that you will look up and behold a new demonstration coming from governments that will take the lead and move in the forefront in this hour," saith the Lord.

"You have entered the hour where the seas of nations will rise up, and judgement will come up out of the waters of the earth. This will be the time that you will hear voices that have never taken the platform before, for they shall come to the forefront to make an announcement that will paralyze the world on the screen."

"The days of laughter shall be many, but the days of tears shall increase. This is the season for you to look at Me and see My glory literally moving you towards a new age in this hour. The churches that you have known in the past will start to decline around their denominational lines. The systems that you have been taught to honor will not be systems of honor any longer, for My glory shall move past the boundaries placed by men who knew Me not," saith the Lord.

"The hour shall come that great political leaders who refused the winds of change will pass off the governmental scene. People and nations will literally call for a shake up within their land, and national securities will be threatened within this season. The days of alliances shall change, and you will see the coming forth of military minds that will start to lead in areas of commerce. Poverty shall be no more as you have known it," saith the Lord.

Taste and See that the Lord is Good

I saw a silver platter appear before my eyes, with delicacies unknown to my eyes. I inquired of the Lord, "Food? Food? Food? What kind of food is this that is coming to the forefront in this hour?" And the Lord said, "I shall cause you to see nations that will end the process of starvation as you know it. It will be the time that you will literally see scientists coming to the platform with cures that will prolong life, but the sense of taste shall be denied."

"The hour shall surely come where there will be a feeding and a diet that will come to the earth, but the physical sense of taste will be denied to men. For I shall break the yoke of gluttony that has shortened the lives of My people, and I shall bring forth a day where you shall see new kinds of meals hitting the marketplace, and they will solve the problem of starvation for entire nations. As knowledge increases rapidly in this hour, the days shall come that you will see life not only prolonged, but you will notice great changes in the community that fights disease. The medical society will start to become overpopulated in its community because of the lack of illnesses. Sickness as you have known. In times past, will change. The days are upon you that you will start to see a new form of doctor coming into place that will conflict with the former form of medical doctors. This will be the rising of a new group of scientists that shall be known as "Preventive Medicine Societies." This group will come forth as a new order of physicians, and they shall be anointed to unlock secrets in the earth concerning foods and bacteria.

"The days will come quickly that diets as you have known them shall take a change. The hours and years shall be long in these arenas, for there will come a time of extreme food poisoning to the bellies of men. This will be the season that you will literally see restaurants and food industries go bankrupt in a matter of days.

"The hour will come swiftly that you will start to see meat coming off of the shelves of grocery stores, and farms shall be stricken in great dilemmas, for the days of meat will be judged in the earth. The animal kingdom will literally rebel because of the power of greed that has entered the nations. I have shaken up the animal kingdom that men have fed poison to because of their own greed, and they shall now feed poison back unto them," saith the Lord.

"Vengeance is Mine, and I am now repaying. The days are upon you that you will start to see a third of the cattle and meat products in your diet start to fall off," saith the Lord. "This is the time that you will see a judgment come upon not only the beef industry, but to all slaughterers who lost the touch of mercy. You will see a disease forming within chicken that will try to spread throughout the populace and the powers that be will try to keep it quiet. But I shall cause the news to leak into the media, and you shall see the days of great upset," saith the Lord. "I bring you to a day of change that will expose the hidden corruption and cancer that lurked within an industry of extreme wealth, for they shall come under the wrath of My judgement, for I am a consuming fire."

The Hour of Transition

The curtains of time drew back before my eyes, and I saw an hourglass suspended in the heavens. An angel stood silent;

holding time in his hand. I asked, "What hour is this?" And
he said, "The hour of transition. The days are here where you
will see seasons and life take on a new shape, and you will literally come to a place that you shall behold the Face of the
Lord that will make you wiser in this hour.

"The power of knowledge will come to the platform, and men
shall move in diverse directions and make discoveries that
will call for attempts of destruction, for entire industries will
collapse overnight. The days are here that God shall send
new deliverers in the earth. They shall come with answers
within them for their generation."

Then I heard the Voice of the Lord saying, "This is the hour
that energy, as you have known it, shall take on a new form.
The questions concerning oil and gas will not only be
answered, but you shall see the dilemma slowly eliminated.
You will become amazed at the resources that I have placed in
the earth for energy," saith the Lord.

"There is a move coming that shall cause knowledge to
increase, and young minds will become the power of the
future. These are they that have come through great tribula-
tion. They are those that had to flee for their own lives while
they were in the womb. These are they that had to come
through the abortion age, and now shall they come to
dethrone the "Herods" and "Pharaohs" that desired to snuff
out their lives," saith the Lord.

"This age shall take out establishments that have threatened
life, and they shall come to the forefront and answer their
foolishness with wisdom that shall remove the evil that has
existed within the nation's systems of destruction and decay,"

saith the Lord.

"The Wish of Death"
I felt myself traveling, and I came to the foot of a majestic mountain, engulfed in the clouds. The mist began to part, and the Lord began to show me the table of nations. Suddenly, a nation emerged that was small in numbers, but mighty in wisdom. And God began to speak:

"You shall see a nation that is small in size and tiny in number according to the estimations of men. They shall appear on the scene with a new kind of war in their hands. These have come to give back to America what America gave to the world. The days of tears will literally be many as a drug will be fabricated from the bosom of this nation, and you will start to see a new addiction that shall come and remove men within an hour. This drug will take men to new heights of pleasure, and then consume them with a sudden destruction," saith the Lord. "It will be known as The Wish of Death."

Emerging Voices
I then saw a swarm of people begin to cover the land. I asked, "Who is this that has come out of the earth?" And God answered, "They are a people that shall be known for their labs and technology. You will see a new kind of war that will make men mock what is now called germ warfare. I will bring you into counsel in this season, and you will start to lift your eyes and see the things that I call you to behold. The hour of prayer will come to the earth. These days will bring key men out of their place of hiding, and voices that didn't want to stand in the forefront will now come to a place of honor and recognition by those who need to hear what I have placed between their lips.

"I will make you wiser than your enemies; than those who know My Name. This will be the hour that I will make men come to a place of walking in revealed knowledge. I will bring you to a season that your eyes shall not only become open, but you will see entire systems fold and new ones emerge. The days of job and work security shall be no more. I will bring you to a place of knowledge and growth.

"Become one of those that I am calling," saith the Lord. "I will direct your paths and affairs. This is the season that I shall make men and women see Me in a degree of light that they have not known. This is the season of great dynamics. I shall cause you to discern the seasons that are upon the earth, and you will witness My Hand in very strange places, for I will appear where men said I would not be, and I shall be moving greatly," saith the Lord.

"I shall make My people that know Me to reveal Me in such astounding ways that the earth shall desire to remove them off My planet. I shall bring forth an order in the earth that will be known for the glory of a new day. This will be the time of a new march, and signals shall resound from on High."

"Make room for the new generals that will come forth from the force of the Elite. I will bring a system into place that shall demonstrate My Name and My glory. I will make you to see a day where mysteries shall be revealed. Those things that you thought were hidden will now start to unveil themselves, and you will find that it was hidden for this new breed to discover."

"I shall call forth a new charge, and you will know that My Voice is mighty. Great shall be My Name! Men shall go places to find My Face, only to discover that My Face is within them. I shall make you wise in many lives, and you will see the Hand of the Lord moving you in directions that will make your life shine."

"It is the day of new light," saith the Lord. "I will cause wisdom to surface in the earth that will cause traditional hearts and minds that appeared stable to think again. It will be known as The Age of Instability, where that which appears off balance will be Me. This is the season of things literally picking themselves up and moving in an orbit that is designed to bring movement for this new day. The battle shall continue, for there shall be men and great groups that will emerge to protect their days of old. I will make you see the change that shall come without the permission of other men," saith the Lord.

"I shall be called **WISDOM** in this hour. I will bring the earth to a standstill in many areas until the sons and daughters that I have elected move into position to set up the next generation of things that shall take mankind into the space age."

"Make room," He said, "for not only will you see Me moving men to the top, but you will not be able to stop nor hold back those who carry My Word in their bellies. These shall bring about the changes that I have ordained and declared that shall be. They will be known as The Fearless and the Daring. I will make their faces as hard as a rock, and many shall literally give their lives for the things that I have called them to bring forth to a system of ignorance."

"The days of light will come that shall prevent darkness from continuing to exist. Make room, for I am moving in the midst of this and I am Mighty. I come to your forefront to make you see Me in ways that will astound you. You shall see Me demonstrate My Face among those who have been called to bear witness of My Name," saith the Lord.

The Mystery of the Prophets

"There shall be the coming forth of a new day, and you will witness the days of My visitation. I will make men who have walked a path of misunderstanding to begin to see My glory appear in arenas that will make men and women have a desire to know Me in an intimate way. I shall bring revelation in this day that will call you to a new place of accountability. The days of great joy will enter into the House of the Lord.

"Prepare, for My Holy Spirit will visit you in this hour, but He will come and speak through men and women that will be special messengers in this age. The days shall come that you will hear the Word of God through them that will point you back to the works of Jesus, and you will acknowledge His glory in a way like you have never known," saith the Lord.

I heard the ticking of a clock reverberate in my ears, and chimes began to toll for a new hour had come. And the Lord began to declare, "Come now, and allow Me to show you the season that is upon the clock." I began to lift up my eyes, and I beheld the hands of the clocks turning backwards. I began to wonder which day the Lord was taking me to, and I desired to come to a place of understanding. The time that I was look- ing for was no more, and the Lord shouted out, "Cease from trying to interpret the season by human hands and human minds, for that is the way of the beast. Come and allow Me to move you in the direction that I have ordained for you to function within."

"Move quickly, for I shall unfold to you why the hands upon the clocks are moving backward. The time of the prophets is dawning, and they shall be special messengers within this hour." I saw children entering the earth in this season and, to my amazement, they stood with what appeared to be diplomas in their hands. I wondered at this vision, and asked, "Why do these possess this type of paperwork?" The Lord said, "Don't you remember what you held in your hands when I sent you to earth?"

My mind went back to the eternal past. I looked up, and there I stood in His Presence with orders in my hand. I began to glance upon the scroll, for what appeared to be a diploma proved to be much more than that. I looked and saw my papers of completion. The papers had already announced my beginning to my end. Hear wisdom! Let him that hath an ear hear what the Spirit is saying to the Church! Let him that has wisdom come before the Lord, and ask Him to teach you how to number your days and apply your understanding to wisdom!

I continued to stand in the Throne Room of Instruction. The Lord said, "Seal up this chapter, and I will open to you the mysteries of the prophets and their assignments in another chapter yet to come. I will cause many out of this book to receive manna that has been hidden for ages. They shall be the company that shall look up and witness the sound of My Voice, and things shall be brought back to their remembrance.

The Lord says, "Make room, for the mystery of God will come to those who are elected to hear it. There will be those who will understand it, and to others it will sound like another tongue for another day. I bring you to a place that you shall discover whether you are of this day or if you should look for another. I will bring forth giants in this hour that will mount up with eagle's wings, and the running will manifest quickly in this day and in this hour," saith the Lord.

"I will make your voice sound out loud, and you will witness the way of thy God. I will make you to fish for My manifestations in this hour. You shall search out the inward parts of your own being, and come to know Me more and more in an intimate way. I will make you wise, and you will begin to sail into a new horizon of understanding like you have never known."

"Make way, for I will now launch you into a new depth. You will start to treasure the gift of God within yourself. I will make you to walk in wisdom, and you shall now enter the new door I bring to you....which is Me. I Am the Door of your understanding; challenging you to come within this realm where there is no end., for there are realms beyond realms. The door you have searched for concerning the mysteries of My Being has left you only at the front door, but I will bring you beyond what you have seen thus far. I declare that it is time for you to move further into the purpose that I have ordained for you to walk in," saith the Lord.

Written Judgments 4

Chapter 2
The Overnight Successes

In this chapter...

The Word of the Lord to Europe 20
The Germs Shall Prophesy 21
The Prophets Shall Speak. 25
The Creator and the Creatures 26
The Waters of Knowledge 27
The Dance of Transformation 29
New Beginnings 30
Alien Communications. 30
Manna From Heaven 32

This is the hour that you will hear laughter on all levels, for this is the time that I shall mock the wisdom of the world. I shall cause men that have operated in their own strength to fall, for they who called themselves developing a life beyond without Me shall find that they will come to nothing. The season of liberty will come in this hour, and you will find the work of God increasing in the earth."

"The days are here that I shall bring forth more healing ministries and ministries that are willing to move in the supernatural without fear," saith the Lord. "I will bring you to a season that you shall see the clear picture for your life in this hour. The days will come quickly that you will start to see the rise of the church in the land."

"I will call some out from amongst the people of the earth, and thou shall hear the prophetic voices I shall call. They shall come standing with much wisdom and discernment. Some will say, 'Who are these overnight successes?' They will come out of remote areas and regions, and the church will literally have meetings to discuss whether these voices operate out from Me or if they emanate from a demonic presence. I will come to you in this hour, and you will come to know My Presence. Those that are the elect shall not be deceived by men or women, for I have given you a divine knower of Truth, which resides in the inner man of the heart."

"I will awaken the things in your heart that desire to manifest in My Presence to be unveiled to you in this hour," saith the Lord. "Come and allow Me to teach you My ways and cause you to know the things that I will place within the earth. Many will come under great scrutiny within the church; especially those in charismatic and independent fellowships. This is the hour that many will start to seek out a covering, but not as you have seen in the past."

"I will cause men that are of Me to join rank with denominational churches. It will be the season that you will see a remarkable degree of unity among these, for this will be the day that each one will teach one. The hour shall come that you will begin seeing Me appear in so many areas that you will stand and say, Can God be in the midst of all of this? I am about to appear to you in ways that will forever amaze you," saith the Lord.

The Word of the Lord to Europe

Then the Lord appeared unto me saying, "Come and allow Me to show you the sea of another nation." The Word of the Lord came unto me saying, "This is the hour for Europe to see My Hand of judgment. Watch for My Hand pointing in a new direction at the same time."

"The hour is coming upon you not only for Europe, but you will start to see currency change on an international basis that will reawaken the level of understanding in My people. I will make you wise in these areas," saith the Lord. "It is the hour that the earth shall receive rain in abundance, and you will start to see a downpour of knowledge that will take the church by storm globally."

"For you say, 'How will all of this effect me in this time?' I bring you into a season of knowing My Voice on many different levels. I will begin to cause men and women to come into the church within this season and they shall learn My ways," saith the Lord.

"These are the days of the truth seekers, and those that will spend time learning My ways shall see the demonstration of My acts with their own eyes. The days will come quickly that you shall both see and hear loud thunders and great flashes of lightning."

The thunders will begin to utter mysteries, and those that understand My plans in this hour shall be able to interpret the voice of the thunders and speak out concerning My ways in this land. I will begin to send messengers in the earth who will bring forth My Voice in the streets. Some will come to remove these that I have sent and discover that they have brought destruction to themselves," saith the Spirit of Truth.

The Germs Shall Prophesy

I stood up in the mountains, and as I looked towards the south, I saw diseases and plagues of every kind. Many could be identified, but even those picked up new strains and had to be redefined before they hit the shores of men's lives. The Word of the Lord came to me saying, "Prepare the earth to answer these germs that have elected to come to the earth in this season.

"I will now cause a new cure to surface, and out of your own plants you will discover that I, the Lord, have moved the mountains so that you could discover the abundance of what I have preserved for you. The hour is fast approaching that you shall see a germ connect itself to poultry, and the price of chicken will so escalate that it will become one of the most expensive meats in the earth. This time I will start to move you towards a meatless diet for a season. The different attacks will start a panic in certain food items, and the economy shall mirror that fear," saith the Lord.

I watched the ocean begin to churn and boil before my eyes. Out of the sea came a fish in North America. I wondered at its appearance, for it was not a fish in our region of the earth. And the Lord said, "I bring new traffic in the sea. I begin to cause a change in the climate, and the seasons of hunting will no longer be as they were before."

"The days will come that children will start to take vaccinations that are quite different from the vaccinations in the sixties and eighties. The children in the New Millennium will be up against the new voices of evolving systems. You will see science run, but they will still try to produce a form of life that will explain the mystery of life."

Overwhelming sorrow filled my heart as I saw tears coming to certain civilizations that helplessly watched loved ones removed from this life through viruses and unexpected diseases. And the Lord said, "This is the hour that you will see great discoveries, but they will come at the expense of mankind. Great will be the price that will be paid by many undeveloped countries. This is the hour that many of your loved ones shall not see the fullness of this day, but they will help others to see the fullness of their days through the unwilling sacrifice of their lives.

"I bring a general to the forefront that will serve time for decisions that were not made by him. He shall volunteer to take the blame for the salvation of that which went undiscovered so that his family and nation will experience freedom. I will cause you to see a day that will be called The Day of Conspiracy, saith the Lord.

"The days will come that a people will rise up and be challenged by the sins of a leader. Things will be shouted at an office that will bring shame upon the leadership of the nation. I will make you wise in this hour, and I shall cause you to see the debates that will manifest behind the scenes of this period," saith the Lord.

"You shall come to a place that a death sentence will be brought to the table to remove not only a man temporarily, but to remove him so that life would not manifest out of his being ever again. New laws shall be put into effect behind the situations. Many will start to serve time long in advance before this leader is tried. This shall be known as the Season of Unforgiveness. I will cause a great amount of media coverage to take place around the world because of the judgment that shall be rendered."

"During this season," saith the Lord, "you will begin to see another government that shall begin to rule and preside over the destiny of a people. Take notice of the emergence of forces that have been in existence for years as they come out of hiding and start a process in America that has never been seen by the face of a people. The days will come that this nation shall suffer the bitter taste of a militant force that will rise out of control, and through this force, many will lose their lives," saith the Lord.

"The days of anarchy shall visit this nation. For out of the days of impeachment will come a force from a people that will be unlike anything that has been seen in the past. This type of terror shall never be seen within the gates of this nation again, for I shall bring you into days that you will find My hand of mercy and laughter outstretched towards thee."

"Wisdom shall visit you in these days. In this season, you will see a new political party that will come to the forefront. You will see untold money creep into this system. It will be the days of entertainment, but great instability in many areas of life. Men shall start to look for stability in areas of life, but they will find none. These will be known as "The Days of Walking Upon Thin Ice."

"The sensation of thin ice will be felt in many areas of life. Some will discover that sudden moves will cause them to experience a sudden collapse, and people shall be moved through fear and control in this season. The forces that will come to power in this hour will be known as "The Forces of Law and Order." When you hear these words frequently, know that it will be the time to weep, for the days of sorrows will be coming a few months after this force is established," saith the Lord.

The Prophets Shall Speak

"I bring you to the days of seeing things appear. You will begin to see the prophets emerging and proclaiming the change of time as you know it. I will cause the turn of the century to be a time that you will see the Hand of the Lord in abject manifestation. It will be known as "The Time of Flexibility." This will be the season that you shall see the nation coming into a time of spirituality. You will mark the days as the days of wisdom that will make you to stand in places and hear wisdom coming out of men that will become great philosophers. I will cause new kinds of education and lectures to come to the forefront in this hour. Make room, for I am moving in the earth. You will see My handiwork in many ways," saith the Lord.

"Come, My people, for I will bring you to a place of learning. See the desires that will start to move you into new areas of thinking and solving life's problems. I will raise up men and women that will make great discoveries in this season. You will see the knowledge of the Lord in demonstration. Make room, for the Day of the Lord will come to visit you, and you shall see Me in ways that you have never known."

Then the Word of the Lord came unto me saying, "Prepare to write the mysteries that I shall bring in your direction this season. I will cause you to move mountains that will make you larger than the life that you have ever known. I will make men and women large and great to see My Face and wonder much about My Grace. It will be the time that you will start to see people relate to Me in ways that will astound you, and you will come to a center of learning that will make one wise.

You will see the glory of the Lord before your eyes and be astonished."

The Creator and the Creatures

I marveled as I saw the Hand of the Lord breaking forth out of the midst of a cloud, for within His Hand were animals caught in His possession. Then the Lord said unto me, "Watch these animals that have been labeled "Creatures of Prey," for they begin to take a different nature and attitude upon themselves, and they shall astound the nations."

Then the Lord said, "Son, come close that you may see the creatures within My Hand. My eyes fell upon the lion, the bear and the eagle. Then I asked the Lord, "What does this mean?" The Lord began to declare, "These are the creatures that have been known to control the world, and many have lauded their great works in the earth, but this is the day that I shall change the guards, and these shall no longer have the rule and honor that they once enjoyed."

I was shocked, and I wondered aloud, "Who shall come to the forefront of power in this hour now if these are toppling from grace?" The Lord said, "Those that I bring to the forefront in this hour shall truly amaze your eyes. This is the hour that you will stagger at My wonders and be overwhelmed by My Grace. The New Millennium will open with a new agenda." I asked, "How will it open?" The Lord replied, "You will see the whole earth and the entire universe testify to what I am about to do in the land.

"The time has arrived that I will cause this age to come and be filled with knowledge that the earth has never seen. You will start to see things moving at an accelerated pace. This will be called "The Age of the Chip." The "chip" will come with much knowledge and information. The age that you shall know will do things in 100 years that would take two millenniums to complete. You will see things accelerate to the point that what should take one thousand years will be completed in one year."

The Waters of Knowledge

"Come to Me so that I can take you to the Well of the Waters of Knowledge, where you can drink of Me and find the answers that you need to know all things." I walked in the Presence of the Lord, and drank of the Waters of Knowledge. It was as if my eyes could now see beyond sight, and I saw nations come to great devastation because of information that was in the "chip" of its day. I saw men making homes in the skies, and below the level of the sea. I saw new governments and powers come into play that amazed me and caused my mind to wonder.

The Lord began to say, "Drink more of the Well of the Waters of Knowledge so that I can bring you to the River of Life." I drank of the cup once again, and my eyes saw creatures that came to us in this realm known as angelic beings. The Lord explained, "The spirit realm and the material realm will start to fuse together as one, for the vibrations upon the earth will make a change because of the minds of men and women will increase the level of their faith in this hour."

I gazed into the Well of Knowledge, and the frothy waters began to giggle as I dipped my cup into them once again. I took another sip, and I looked up and saw uninhabited places literally become cities of refuge. And the Lord said, "This is the hour that you will see islands come forth, for the lands of the seas will be developed. This is the time that you will see the fulfillment of My Word, and you will witness the islands of the seas become as strong cities. This is the hour that you shall see degrees of construction and redevelopment that will literally astound you. This will be known as "The Age of Strong Cities." This is the season of an age of development that will cause men to take up new studies in the area of architectural design."

I peered into the well again, and the waters began to murmur amongst themselves, "Who is this man who drinks of us? He's tasting of our mysteries." I dipped my cup yet again, and the waters became silent. Then the Lord said, "You will see even more of My knowledge." It seemed as though my eyes were ablaze with the Glory of the Lord, and the Vision of the Lord consumed me. I saw transportation taking a new identity upon itself. And God said, "This will be the day that you shall see the heavens fill with men. It will be the time that man shall take off as the fowl of the air. This is the time that you will find answers to the large problems of the cities. The field of transportation will take on a new destiny, for I will cause life to move at a pace that will amaze the natural minds of men."

"This is the time that you shall see a new kind of energy come into the market place. I will meet you in realms that will cause your mind to see me in ways that you have never known. I will make you to see wisdom, so that what men will call evil, you will recognize as Me. They do not understand the moving of My Hand, and they will not see Me in familiar dimensions. The days will shoot forth that you will see a new kind of being coming into the earth. It will be the time that science will go into territory that man shall call "The Forbidden

Zone." It will be in this season that you will begin to wonder how much of everything that is happening is of Me. But I declare unto you that it is all Me. I will cause you to see My glory in everything in this hour," saith the Lord.

The Dance of Transformation

My ears were thrilled with the sudden strains of a hauntingly beautiful melody, and I looked up and saw a dance in the heavens of creatures of every kind. The Lord then said, "This is the hour that men have come to, and it is the next season in which I have ordained for them to walk. I shall now cause them to see world rulers come to the platform in this hour."

As the dance continued, I began to see new governments form out of the partnerships of the Dance of Transformation. They were formed at land and were formed at sea. The Lord said, "Come and allow Me to show you the technology that shall come to homes around the world that shall prepare men to see My Glory and My coming in the air."

"Television screens will not have the same shape, and their sizes will be different. This will be known as the season that men will go to trade in the machines that they had bought in the past to get the new machine that will give a cleaner and clearer picture. At this time, media shall take a new turn, and you will see cultures and countries possess their own programming for the world to see. It will be the time that you will come to know the Face of the Lord that shall bring those in the background to the forefront in this hour," saith the Lord.

"The days of preaching shall be many, but you will see all kinds of men and women declaring Me in different forms and by different Names. I will bring you counsel in this hour, and I shall give you great wisdom. Do not debate with anyone concerning Me, for I have not called you to defend Me nor My Name, for I AM that I AM. Just do the miracles and the works that I have told you to do, and that will be honor within itself," saith the Lord.

"The days will come that I will show you the false prophets. The false prophets are those that testify of Me but do not do the works that I tell them to do. The days are forthcoming that you will start to see men and women coming to the earth to work miracles and do My works, but yet they will be individuals of very few choice words," saith the Lord.

New Beginnings
"This will be known as "The Age of Action and Less Talking." I will declare My Glory through those that have looked upon Me and showed the world what they beheld as they saw Me. I will make men to grow life in the earth that has not had a platform. You will start to see a beauty in plant life that will come forth through a saint that will demonstrate My beauty out of the vegetable kingdom.

"The days will come that you will see plants come alive in your realm through drama. New characters will come forth that will bring new definition to those that will be entertained by them. I will bring plants alive as I have brought animals alive in your realm," saith the Lord.

Alien Communications
"You will be visited in ways in the earth through satellite, and the days will come that a communication will be picked up and transmitted to the earth. It will cause a concern in the

nations, and media will take it beyond measure and, out of fear, they will make an erroneous announcement. They will not understand the interpretation nor the symbolism of these beings," saith the Lord.

I asked the Lord, "Who are these beings that will come to us from afar?" And He said, "They are angels. They are messengers that will be sent to earth to show you My Glory. Men will call them "the devil" because they do not understand Me nor My ways."

"While moving in this hour will be a day of new beginnings, I will make you to operate in wisdom and you will see the Reward of the Lord in this hour. This will be a time that you will start to witness My righteousness on many levels that will make you understand My plan for the ages."

"Now is the time for new creativity to come forth. I will make you to understand My internal plan within your life. I will cause a new generation that is entering the earth to be wiser and greater in their ability to move life light years ahead of this present age. I will make you see the wonder of My Face and the days of My Glory. I will enlarge you in this hour, and you will excel in the learning that you have received."

"I will make you see Me with eyes of intelligence that you have never known. I am calling you to a new definition. I will make you accountable to learn the ways in which I am moving, and you will come to know Me on many different levels," saith the Lord. "I will show you My plan for your life, and you will make a new day come alive in your situation. I will cause you to understand the walk to which you will be called. Come to the place where you can walk by faith and not by sight," saith the Lord.

Manna From Heaven

"Now is the time to look towards Me as the Ancient of Days. I will take you to see the future by showing you My back parts," saith the Lord. "For all the things that you call "future" are behind you. I will make you wise to the point that you shall come to a new understanding of Who I am, and you will make some major moves that will bring you into the land that I have ordained," saith the Lord.

"Now is the time that I will cause you to be caught up in My Presence. This will be the time that I will give you new definition. Make room for the abundance that is coming forth in this hour! I will cause money to make its way into your lives, for a new currency will start to come in your direction that will make you wise in the distribution of your own wealth," saith the Lord.

"Now is the time for you to make a new launch into the future. You must understand the plan that I have for your lives. I will make you to understand why your life shall unfold the way that it is moving. This is the hour that you will not know suffering as you have known it in the past, for I will cause a new food to develop that will eliminate starvation from the earth. But there shall be countries that will still experience starvation, for the hearts of men are wicked. I will show you this, and you will see nutrition come to you in a capsule, and many will wonder how all their energy is met. I will feed you again as I did Israel in the wilderness with the manna from on High. This manna will be a mystery in the earth, and men will say, "What is it?"

This manna will cause men to come up with definitions that will satisfy the public, but at large, they will not know how it works or what makes it hold the human body together for ages. This capsule will be known to many as "The Eternal Food." Some will even call it "The Diet of Angels." But out of all that they call it, I will keep revealing the mystery of My Will. I shall cause you to see My Hand in many unusual ways that will bring joy and laughter to you," saith the Lord.

Now, as we come to the close of this chapter, let us prepare for the judgements that are written to ages that are without an end.

Written Judgments 4

Chapter 3
The Mystery of Destiny

In this chapter...

The Birth of a Prophet. 35
The Word of the Lord for America 37
The Unfinished Symphony Will Be Finished . . . 40
Revelations From the Heavenlies 41
The Mysteries of His Will. 42
The Fruit With No Name 45
The Prophet in the Riddle 46

Come now, and allow Me to show you the Mystery of Destiny. I will bring you the answers to questions that have been veiled since the beginning of time as you know it," saith the Lord. "Now I come to show you the birth of a people which is the birth of a prophet." The Lord began to take me to what appeared to be a High Place. He showed me a realm where time was no more. Out of this day came forth a sound and music unlike anything that could be described on this plane.

The Birth of a Prophet
I asked the Lord, "What is this sound? What is the music that I hear?" The Lord declared, "It is the sound of the instructions that I seal within the ears of men, for they must know their assignments and the day of destiny that awaits fulfillment in the earth. This is the time for you to know how the prophet receives his call and My plan for a people and a nation."

Then the Lord took me to another pinnacle, and showed me a generation that had come before, another generation that is coming now, and finally a generation that will come; yet they are all the same generation. I looked up to try to make sense out of what I was seeing so that I could declare it, only to note that there is only one generation that makes it to the earth. Everything is nothing but a repeat of time over and over again, for you see, time mirrors the one way in which Jesus Christ is the same yesterday, today and forever.

Then the Hand of the Lord came unto me saying, "This is the time that you will see the continuation of those things which I have started, and you will see the end of a day and a great period arising in this hour. I make you wise in the things that I call you to do, for it is the hour of the gathering of what men call "new information," but I will declare unto you that it is information that always was. It is now being unveiled to those that have ears to hear what the Spirit is saying to the Church.

"I bring you aside that I may teach you the things that you have forgotten. You see," saith the Lord, "this is the purpose of the Holy Spirit, for I come to bring all things back to your remembrance. There is nothing new under the sun. All that you need to know you already know. It is just the time for you to step back and remember that which I have already imparted unto you."

I looked up, and I saw the School of the Prophets. It was a place prepared in the mind of God since the beginning of time. The Lord began to declare to me that His plan was to always have His Voice in the earth through beings that were willing to make the necessary announcements in different periods of time. I asked, "Why do you call them "beings?"

The Lord answered, "I call them "beings" because I speak through all things in all times. These are the prophets of the day of the Lord. I prophesied through Balaam's ass. I have spoken through ravens and doves when My people needed to hear My Voice in times of direction. I spoke through winds and seas. Behold, for these are the prophets of God– these are they that will carry out My will, and accurately declare what I am doing in the earth."

"Prepare yourself, for you will start to see men come forth that the world shall declare, "These are before their time." But I will have you to know that they always were, and you are appointed among that company," saith the Lord.

The Word of the Lord for America

Then the Lord took me up, and as we soared through the heavenlies, He caused me to see from realms that I had never seen before. He took me to what I would call "back" in order to see forward to the Day of Destiny and the plight of America and the American people.

He began to utter, "Now is the time that you will see a government exchange power that will be for the people for a force that will change the election process in America as you now know it. It will be the day that you will look up and mourn, "Where is the freedom for which many have fought?" You will now see the time clock begin to accelerate, and My judgement shall be quick."

"I shall cause men to fall to their knees in prayer, and they shall see My Face in dimensions that they have never seen Me before. I call them to become accountable for the things that they have laid down. The days will come that you will see the

Church change its method of worship, and the institutions that are in the earth called "Houses of God" shall take on a new look. Their calling shall be more profound than that which any generation has ever known."

"The days will come that these institutions will become strong power bases of influence, and these days will come quickly into view," saith the Lord. "I bring you to a place of new hours, and times that you have never known. I call you to a day of awakening, but the country you have seen will not be the country that you have known."

Then I looked to my right, and I saw entire states breaking off from the United States of America, angrily demanding their freedom from a Constitution that was set in place by laws that appeared to be unbreakable. It was a day of sudden upheaval. I looked to the Lord, and asked, "Why are these days approaching? This cannot be happening in the country of Liberty!" The Lord said, "The hourglass has run out, and this land will now be rushed into its next season of destiny. Behold the little books that individuals are carrying." I looked down into the hands of a people, and I asked, "What meanest this?" The Lord said, "It is a passport. The days will come that you will need a book to travel from one state to the next in order to gain entrance within their gates."

"The hour will come that you will see a nation that was once united become drastically divided. The Lord began to say to me, "You will only see the ripple beginning, but the fullness of these things will take place in the lives of spirits that will come to earth to bring the nation into its next season of destiny."

I asked the Lord, "Why was this coming about?" He declared, "You have both heard and read My law, yet you ask "Why this?" Did I not say that whatsoever a man soweth that shall he also reap? I do not change My mind or plan when it comes to the accountability of nations. I will now bring a judgement upon this nation that she has brought to different parts of the earth. You will see the days that families will be divided over state lines, and it will be the hour of great weeping and regret."

"But I now call you to a new day," saith the Lord. "This will begin to take place over groups that will start to bring up issues concerning the Constitution. There will be a major law school that shall emerge in time that will release into a system those that shall be known as free radicals."

"The hour is approaching that you will start to see people migrating to different parts of the country, and you will see a time that lights will be forced out in certain communities. I now make you to move in wisdom, and you shall know My Face in a way that you have never known. It will be the time that I shall call you to recognize the Presence that I am in the earth."

"I shall, in this season, show you My will, and My mercy will be brought forth in this hour. I will change the tax system as you know it. There shall be great persecution that will sweep the land in this hour, and great shall be the fall of many," saith the Lord.

"This is the hour that you will make known My mystery. I will begin to clear those that desire to see My Light. I will make them wise in this hour, and you shall come to know My glory in this season. You will become aware of a new sense of destiny," saith the Lord.

"Wake up and behold the hour that I bring you to a place of being. You will see not only My Face, but you shall know My Name. I bring you to a place of peace and satisfaction. I now call you to a new day of revelation. I shall reveal My Son in you as you are willing to show Me in the earth. The hour is now upon you that you will see the prophets coming to the forefront to make announcements about the mystery of God. The religious church will have problems with their message, but it will provoke them out of their comfort zones," saith the Lord.

"Prepare! For you will see a battle in the minds of men that will cause a war with their lower and higher nature. They shall begin to battle with their conceptions of what is of the Lord and what is not. I shall bring you to a place that you will see a company emerge that will understand the Spirit of Revelation, which is the Spirit of the Lord.

"The days are quickly coming forth that you will hear a new sound coming to the earth. This sound will start the procession of new voices that are called by the Master in this hour to sound the trumpet in the earth. Come now, and let us hear what they will come saying in their day," saith the Lord.

The Unfinished Symphony Will Be Finished
"This is the season to lift thyself from the place of comfort, and hear the messengers that have been sent to complete the unfinished symphony. I heard them declare the same Word as the prophets of old. They came with a sound that was articulate, and their voices brought people into a state of conscious-

ness where they were mesmerized by their message. This is the hour that I will anoint My prophets with the gift of an orator, and I shall cause them to prophesy. They will announce the destruction of cities and countries that will be called to their end in their season," saith the Lord.

"This will be "The Hour of the Roll Call." The prophets will come to the earth and announce those that are to remain and be finished within this system, as you know it. I will now bring you to a day that I will wipe out certain names from the earth. I will not allow any boys to come out of their loins, and I will make them the final generation of their day. Others I will take and render sterile, and I will allow no children to proceed from them. I shall remove them in their day, for their names have come up on the roll call, and they are finished from this realm."

The Lord continued to speak, "You will see Me wipe out entire nations in a day, only to make ready a new people. I will cause things to come upon the earth that will start to call men, cities, and nations out in their entirety. The hour is upon you that you will see the Face of the Lord in ways and means that you have not known.

Revelations from the Heavenlies
"I will make a generation that will accurately announce My will. There will be prophets in this hour that will come to stand in the way of what I am doing by asking for mercy, but there shall be no mercy," saith the Lord. "I will cause an hour to come that will make it "The Hour of Trumpets." You will hear of strange things in the heavenlies. Out of this day shall I bring you signs in the earth, which will cause men to literally lose their minds, for they will not be able to explain the phe-

nomena of things that I shall bring forth."

"I shall bring a sound out of the heavens that will cause men to hear Me in every nation, kindred, and tongue. There will be a sound that shall be interpreted from the heavens in a day that shall cause much news coverage. Of course, that which is called "The Church" will have great problems in this day. They will be split over whether this is of Me or not. But I will show you a mystery. I will only cause the earth to get a glimpse of the heavens declaring My glory, but in a way that will be quite profound in its day," saith the Lord.

The Mysteries of His Will

"Now move to the side, and allow Me to show you the days of greater glory and newer heights. I make you wise in the mission that you are called to fulfill in this hour. The hour is upon the earth that you will see unusual changes in the climate that will bring much interest to those who will witness My Hand."

The air began to rustle, and I heard the distinct sounds of muffled voices, but I could see no one before my eyes. And the Lord said, "The Hour of Whispering shall come into the earth. This is the hour that you will literally see and hear men whispering the mysteries of My will. This is the day that you will be made aware of the things that I am doing and saying. I will bring together a company that will be called "The Elect." They will be individuals who will know My Name, and they will whisper the mysteries of My Kingdom to one another."

"I will bring churches to the forefront that will come to their hour of deliverance. It will be the time that you will see those that are called of Me come to a place of fulfilling Destiny by meeting Spirits of Destiny. I now bring the Church to a day of new terms. You will hear words that will amaze you, and many will come to the table discussing what is allowed and what is not. It will be the time of the emergence of new "Sanhedrins" and courts that will judge the religious systems of this day."

"I will make you see Me in a dimension that will make you wise to your calling and purpose in this hour," saith the Lord. "You will start to see many things coming to the forefront in this hour that will make you know that My glory is in the midst of you and it is mighty to save, heal and deliver."

"Now is the season for you to step wisely in all the things that I call you to do. This is the hour that prophets will start to seek out their instructor in this realm. They will come to know who their teachers are and find them while in their assignment or on their way to a mission. I will bring clarity to the prophets' office, and the mantle in this season will be quite profound", saith the Lord.

"Let him that has wisdom know that all things must be taught if they want to become a teacher; for it takes one to know one. Unless a teacher has his hand on you, it is illegal to place your hands upon a student. You can only impart what you are, and in order to become; a master in the realm you wish to develop must first touch you."

"Now the hour shall come that a company shall walk in great misunderstanding declaring, "We are of that people that need no man to teach us, for we are taught by the Holy Ghost." "Well," saith the Lord, "that company will be short lived as an example of what happens to those that circumvent My law. I will bring forth those whom I have called by My Name. These are they that shall not see their teachers as mere men and women, but they will see that they are the Holy Ones sent from above."

"Man is not a being of flesh. Man is a lower nature of Spirit that ascends to the fullness of being which is Divine Sonship. I will make these things plain to those that will have an ear to hear what the Spirit of the Lord is saying to the Church. I now make you to come to a place of Divine Order, and you will start to move forward in time like never before."

"Come to a place of clear thoughts and purpose, and I shall bring you peace," saith the Lord. "I will make you wise as a serpent in this hour. I now call you to a new day of impartation. I will bring to account those that will have a new sense of responsibility. This will be known as "The Time of a Focused Company," for these men and women will make My purpose clear in this hour."

"I will make you see the counsel of the Lord. This is the time for you to start to reap new benefits that will come your way. I will make a people that have been weary to find a time of new refreshing. I will bring your eyes to see the Word of the Lord fulfilled in your ears," saith the Lord.

"This is the hour that you will get a new vision of the nations of the world. I will make you come to a place of "clear seeing." I will make the eyes of the prophets so clear, that many will run in amazement saying, "Hide us from these seers!"

"There is a company of seers coming forth that will see through men and women with great insight. Now is the Call of Destiny. I will make you understand the plan and arrangements of unsettled issues that are at hand. I will call you to give a new account of the scales that are in the earth," saith the Lord.

"I will bring leadership into a new place of responsibility, for they will start to bring forth answers to communities and lives in many different arenas. The cures of diseases shall begin to manifest themselves in ways that are unlike any time of recorded history. It will be the time of healing past wounds and hurts. There will be a people that will surface through the mud and sorrows of life."

The Fruit With No Name
"I will call you to record today that I will make you to wise up in all the things that you do. Make loud the sound of great ability, and move into the next day of understanding. I will allow you the pleasure of tasting the fruit of a day that has not yet been born in this realm, but always was since time began."

A being appeared before me, and placed fruit in my hand that I did not recognize, and told me to take and eat. God began to speak and said that I now held in my hand answers to all the world's problems. I asked, "Where did this fruit come from? It looks familiar but yet it tastes strange to me." I asked the Lord, "What is in this fruit?" The Lord answered again, "It is the solution to all of man's problems and the answers to every question that exists in the universe." I asked the Lord to give me the name of the fruit, and He did, but He commanded me, "Do not write it. For in the day that man realizes this fruit and its name, he will continue to abuse it and use it for destructive purposes and not for the purpose that can bring hope and peace to the earth."

The Prophet in the Riddle

Then the clouds began to gather and declare, "Give way to those that shall come that are worthy of this message." Then the Lord began to make an announcement. "They have already heard this message. Remember that they were in the School of the Prophets from the beginning of time. Behold, for now is the time that I shall raise up prophets that will come with riddles to make known the Word of the Lord through the riddles that they will echo," saith the Lord.

"Take hold of the wisdom that I am declaring. For there is only one generation that comes to earth, and it is the same generation. They will come knowing the hour and the day that Destiny will make wisdom so simple that even the fool in heart will learn if they have a desire to know and understand My plan, saith the Lord."

"I am dwelling in your midst at this hour in the form of wisdom and age."

Chapter 4
Locate Wisdom

In this chapter...
The Dance of Mystery 48
Breaking All Codes of Silence 48
Broken Vows. 49
The Protein Agenda 50
The Future in the Present 50
The Voice of Louisiana 51
The Time of the Great Dance 52
The Shaking of the Lord in Australia 53
Prophecy to South Africa. 53
The Millennium of Transportation. 55
Progress in Education. 56
Secret Mysteries Revealed 58

Find Me, saith the Lord! "Find Me," saith the Lord. "Look out and see if you can locate Me, for I am in your earth. So find Me! I am not lost, but I am only hidden to those that cannot see Me. Open now your eyes and behold Me, for I am here speaking and declaring to you all the time," saith the Lord.

"This time I come to you in wisdom and in riddles. I will cause you to know the hours that are set before you and the realm that you have been called to fulfill in this day. You will start to see the unveiling of My Face. I will bring you to a point of witnessing My great grace, and the abundance that you desired will make you wise in this hour."

"Now I will cause you to find the treasures that are in the earth. They are located in the dark realms that man would call "Forbidden." I will bring you to a place of counsel, and you will start to visit on a new plane and experience My honor in ways like you have never known. Come to a place of results! You will see Me moving in your lives, and the days of striving will cease as you enter the realm that I shall call "Peace," saith the Lord.

The Dance of Mystery

"Come now, and allow Me to show you the mountains moving out of their places." I began to watch the mountains begin a dance of mystery. And the Lord said, "The days of media shall see a drastic change. The days of freedom in the media shall experience the yoke of new regulations. These days will visit the nations because sensitive issues shall come to the forefront, and abuses will surface in the area of information."

"Your eyes shall see the handwriting upon the walls in many areas. The hour will come that you will see leadership trying to mop up a situation that will literally bring disaster to those that have moved in a lack of wisdom in the destiny of their day. I will show you the honor that I shall bring to those that shall become accountable in this hour. I will show you many that will make large advancements. This is the hour for you to see the breaking of the seals in the nation."

Breaking All Codes of Silence

"The time that you now know in the New Millennium will be known as "Breaking All Codes of Silence." Everything that has been done in silence shall come to the light. You will see the Word of the Lord penetrating to the core of the matter, and computers will vomit up the information that they have been commanded to eat and digest. It will be as if a virus shall come in the time of information and cause everything that was kept down to regurgitate to the forefront in this hour," saith the Lord.

"Prepare for the move that I will make in your midst. This is the season to watch My Hand moving across the airwaves in an unprecedented way. I will make them wise that will hear wisdom. You will see children rise up in classrooms, and you will see a teacher murdered in a classroom. This will start new laws to be set on the books, and will initiate new cycles and trends in the entire educational system.

"During this season, you will hear the voices of child abuse fighting with the voices of corporal punishment. This will be known as "A Season of Anarchy." I will make you see the way that I am moving in this hour," saith the Lord.

Broken Vows

There was silence for what seemed an interminable time as I pondered the judgments I had seen and heard. I felt a solemnity that sat upon my mind like a blanket, when suddenly I heard a Voice screaming in the heavenlies saying, "Now is the time for the germs to gather and judge mankind for not keeping their vows to one another." I began to move with great haste to get an understanding of what was coming to the earth. Then I heard the Voice saying, "Prepare cattle and water to withhold themselves from the feeding of men." Then the Lord said, "Man has violated the laws of life, and for this cause, a day shall come that man will pay for the sins he committed against the lives of animals and rivers."

"Now this is the time for you to witness clarity and a new sense of destiny. You will start to see industries running for cover. The days will come that you will find very little milk in the land that will be safe for human consumption." I looked up, and I saw another industry beginning to collapse. Then the milk and dairy industries came to a sudden standstill. Men were looking for ice cream and could find none.

And the Lord said, "This is the time that you will make some new progress in the areas of food. It will be the time called "The Slaughter of Cattle." These will be known as "The Days of Great Slaughter." The land will mourn, for billions of dollars will leave the economy and a new appetite will suddenly emerge on the scene. This will come at a very inconvenient time in history.

The Protein Agenda
"The days will come that you will see hospital stations filled up with men and women getting shots to place protein in their body. Great will be the industry of nuts in this hour. The demand will become so high that many will succumb to greed and set ridiculous prices upon that which is common to the earth. The prices will be so high that it will be a sin to buy from them," saith the Lord. "New laws will be passed in the land to set a limit upon what men can charge for items of necessity."

The Lord continued, "Now is the time that you will start to see Me multiply in your midst. Make room, for I am moving in the earth. This will be the season that I will visit you in ways that will make you understand My plan for humanity and the system that will work for men if they work with Me."

The Future in the Present
"The time will come that you will make known the vision that I have for those that will discover who I am in this hour. Now

is the time to move into a season known as "The Time of Clearing the Air." This will be the season that a new energy will force itself to the marketplace. Cars will run on a different type of fuel and energy than what has been known in the past. It will be known as "The Time of Moving Forward Into Destiny." The future will bring some simple answers to complex situations. This will be known as an age that will pull people into a new cycle of the future," saith the Lord.

"I now move you into the realm of Destiny that will start to solve problems for many that have been caught up in transitory situations. This is the time that you will see the Writing of God appearing across the skies in airlines and carriers that will literally stop at new international ports. This will be the season of the severe changing of the guards."

The Voice of Louisiana
"You will see companies moving in the avenues of major takeovers, and there shall be much sabotage in the area of information. I will cause a wisdom to come out of a remote place, and a state that has no recognition will come to the front of time with answers to a complex situation that will rise out of the nation. This will be the state of Louisiana, and her destiny awaits fulfillment."

"There will be a great deliverance coming to the nation when you see a voice come to the platform out of the state of Louisiana. This will be the voice of a great speechmaker. He will lead the nation into a season of freedom. He will challenge a system out of this place and bring many enemies out of hiding. The voice of the oppressed will also be heard during this season."

"This leader will have an attempt made upon his life. He will be the one that will make a great mark in history and restore what kings tried to bring to pass in these parts. I will begin to unlock the Mystery of Memphis in the turn of the century. I will bring much attention to this part of the country. The year 2003 will be the season of a new birth, and a people that have cried for liberty will see their day and call it "Freedom," saith the Lord.

The Time of the Great Dance
"Now, you will make some moves in this hour that will give nations around the world tremors that will literally shake economies to the core. Now will be "The Time of the Great Dance." Move forward into action!" As I stood gazing, angels came from all around joyously singing, "Salvation has come to men again!" And the Lord said, "This is the season that you will start to make great strides in history. The information age will move rapidly. It will be the time that you will see technology become a period of great trade-ins."

The time will come that you will see the dawn before the morning. This will be known as "The Emerging of the Great Mind of the East." This is the day that many children of the west will move eastward for their education, and the days of learning will go into reverse. The days of great education will begin to dwindle, and the minds of the west will no longer hold the torch of learning for the world."

"Great institutions will come out of Asia and Africa. These will be the days you will see men going back to the soils of their beginnings, and they will uncover answers for the great civilizations that will take the stage in this hour," saith the Lord.

My eyes began to tear as I saw a great city buried under the rubble and dust of a shaken foundation. I began to wonder, "Where is this city?" The earth suddenly moved under my feet, and I would not dare to make a move. This disaster came to a place without warning, and the Lord said, "This is the time of earthquakes in divers places."

The Shaking of the Lord in Australia

The nation of Australia came to my mind, and the Lord said, "Prepare them next for the agenda that has come to the table." Then I heard the Voice of the Lord taunting, "So you have thrown the rocks, but hid your hand. I shall bring your sins out of hiding. Where are the people of the land that I have placed upon the earth? Where have you driven them? I shall visit you quickly, and you will see My Hand by 2010," saith the Lord.

"I will visit your economy, and you will come to a sudden stop because of the harboring of like minds within your borders. I will make your monies scarce, and you will look for gold and shall find none. Many will look for your currency and laugh at it. The days will come that your money will become mockery to the other nations of the world. This is the hour that you will literally wonder what has happened overnight. I come swiftly to bring you your just reward," saith the Lord.

Prophecy to South Africa

The Word of the Lord came unto me saying, "I am coming in the midst of South Africa as a swift wind. I will make known My wisdom among that people in this hour. I will cause you to see the fulfillment of My purpose among that people. I will bring people from around the world to behold My doings," saith the Lord.

"I will now say unto you that you will start to see great churches spring forth out of the village. You will look in amazement at My handiwork. I will cause a lot of noise to be made out of the midst of that people. It will be the season that you will see great wonders and pioneers coming forth from among the people of God."

"This will be the hour that I shall visit that nation with Christian television. You will see a God-fearing people emerge, and you will come to a new knowledge of a Christian nation. I will make wisdom to shine through mighty men and women of God. They will travel to the continents of the earth, and proclaim liberty to those that are bound in sin."

"I will establish their voices around the world, even in North America. You will see them coming to bring a message of reconciliation and establishment. This will happen, but it shall come out of the natives of the land," saith the Lord.

"I must show you the clock upon the wall. It is the hour that fuel prices will start to endure some unusual changes in prices. There shall be a government in power that will collapse because a day is coming that the world will turn its back on fuel, and you will see this nation as a nation of power no more," saith the Lord.

"This will be the season that the world will take on a new color. The way of travel shall change rapidly. It will be the hour that you will literally start to see the celebration of God in inventions. I will make a generation wise in this age that will come forth with a mighty word and wisdom. The hour shall now come that you will literally come to a place of new accountability."

The Millennium of Transportation

"Now come and allow Me to show you the coming forth of an industry that will take upon itself a new look. I will show you millenniums beyond this," saith the Lord. I began to travel in time, and I beheld men and women transported by a means of transportation that could not be described. It was a day whereby man moved about and traveled at the speed of thought."

And the Lord said, "This is the hour that I shall give you a glimpse of those things that will shortly come to pass. You will start to see a great turnover in industries that will begin to soar and bring great ability to man in this hour. I will make you wise in this day to understand My plan, and you will see the breaking forth of a brand new day and season of joy."

"I will cause you to stand in amazement as you see the days of invention. The days will come that airlines will no longer have the same look. The speed of travel in the air will become faster and faster. It will be the day that commercial airlines will take upon themselves a new look. What took three hours to travel will start to be accomplished within an hour."

"You will start to see trips manifest from one destination to the next within the self-same hour. Then you will come to understand that which I came declaring unto you in the days that I walked your earth as a man, and worked miracles within the self-same hour. This will be but a taste of some of the greater works than these that you shall do."

"I will move you about in this hour, and you will see entertainment change in the skies. You will see gambling in the air. You will see all kinds of things starting to take on a new look in this hour," saith the Lord. "I will make you wise in this hour to understand the things that I am doing in the earth."

"This will be the time that you will make way for new days. You will see games in the skies and at home that will cause men and women to lose a great deal of money. You will see entertainment centers come into the home that will appear to be innocent, but for the undisciplined individuals, plenty of money will be wasted and lost. The days will come that you will see men placing bets upon games by way of television, and a great deal of debate will come about concerning these issues," saith the Lord.

"You will see some of these things legalized in some states and rejected in others. I will make you see the plans of earth unfold, and you will start to see many riddles unlocked within this hour. I will cause you to see the earth rapidly evolve. It shall prepare itself for the great minds that will be coming forth. I will make you so wise in these days that you'll start to come to a new understanding concerning My plan for the ages.

Progress in Education

"Make room, for I will cause you to see My workings among you in the area of education. I will remove the classroom setting out of buildings as you now know them. This will be the time that you will see more people working out of their homes. It will be the season that you will see children sign in and take courses over computer terminals and just appear at certain centers of learning for scoring and testing," saith the

Lord.

"The days will come that you will see remarkable young geniuses come forth, and it will be the hour that science and mathematics will take on a new look and trend. I will take you to a place of new creativity. It is the day that you will take on a new look in this hour. You will stand and declare the Word of the Lord to many people. I will make you stand in doors that will literally amaze you and bring you to a new confidence."

"This is the hour that you will make new progress in many areas. The days of service will change rapidly. You will see more and more nations that have been undeveloped become developed nations. This is the hour for you to make room, for travel will be much in this hour. I will have you stand in the doorways of opportunity."

"This is the hour for you to seek My Face, for I will bring you wealth from areas that will amaze you. I will show you that money will start to come from your ability to think and dream. I will have you make new appointments with the economy. The days will come that the developed nations will celebrate only the working minds. This will be the hour that you will see the rich only coming out of the minds of great inventors," saith the Lord.

"The days will come quickly that you will start to see a new kind of sport enter the arena of entertainment. The popularity of baseball, basketball, hockey, and other kinds of sports entertainment that amuses the present generation will decline in a generation that will amaze you. It will start with a strike that will be without end. It will be in this season that you will start to see My Word fulfilled in many ways," saith the Lord. "This is the hour that you will start to see entertainment take upon itself a very primitive type of beguilement and men and women will look for actual blood to be drawn."

Secret Mysteries Revealed

"There will be amazing discoveries in the area of after-death experiences. There shall be some things that will bring great upset to the public at large. This will be the resurrection of a body through science, and they will tell stories about the scenes they have experienced on the other side."

"Out of this, I shall move among mankind, and you will find that the sting of death shall be lost and men will look forward to the opportunity to pass into the next life. I will remove the mystery from death, for that has been the sting. The sting is the ignorance and fear of the unknown. I will cause men to walk in the realm of awareness, and time will move at great speed," saith the Lord.

"During this season, you will see the life span extended. Men and women will live longer and longer. It will be the time that Social Service, as you know it, will collapse. A new kind of money will surface and come to the forefront. I will make you to understand wisdom in this hour that will make things accelerate at a higher pace than you have ever known. It will be the days of longevity in many areas and directions. I will cause you to see Me moving in the midst of you, and life will take upon itself a new turn," saith the Lord.

"Now is the time for you to make room for the enlargement that is coming in your direction. I will cause issues concerning life to come to the table. It will be the time of new discoveries, and laughter will come to many that will take a stand to move in the direction of righteousness. Come now, and allow Me to show you your diet, and you will start to see why men shall live long and be satisfied in their old age."

"New forms of worship will begin to come to the earth in this hour that will force men and women to take another look at their lives and their worship of God. This will be the days of understanding and clarity, and people will run to get the knowledge of Me in great ways," saith the Lord.

Chapter 5
The New Order

In this chapter...

The Tax System 61
Black Colleges in America. 63
The Enslavement 63
The Weather Shall Prophesy. 64
The Nations Shall Rebel 64

The Word of the Lord came unto me saying, "This is the time for you to view the New Order that is coming into the earth. I will bring you to a new season of sight, and you will begin to find Me in unusual places. It will literally surprise you that there could be a move of God within those walls."

The Tax System

"I will cause you to see laws and systems crumble, and you will begin to see an old guard moving from the front of the line to the rear," saith the Lord. "I will cause you to see a judgment come to the tax system as you understand it. I will make you wise in this hour, and you will see new tax laws coming forth that will lend themselves to helping people in the United States to live a finer and greater quality of life."

"This is the hour that you will start to see a decline in the prison system as you now understand it. It will be the time that you will see the nation moving in the direction of morality. I will cause you to view Me in ways that will start a procession and gathering of My people together. You will start to see a nation beginning to take on a new look and approach concerning world policies."

"This is the hour that you will start to see oppressed people coming out of their houses of bondage. This is the time for you to experience an elevation," saith the Lord. "I will make this the hour that you will witness My plan, for a people that I have brought out of dilemmas have become bound more and more."

"You will now come to a place that you will start to see leaders coming together out of different communities. They will lay aside their differences and start to bring a people together that will move out of the lack and confusion that has existed in their midst."

"I bring you to a new place of understanding, for this is the time you must become wise in many decisions that you shall make. I will cause you to consider the days of turning. You will see women coming forth in larger numbers as activists, and you will start to see great women moving in this hour that will have the spirit of Esther. They will know that they have been born for such a time as this."

"Consider what great matter has been set before you. I will make you wise in the discovery of conditions that will come to a people, for this will change lives and education as you understand it. This is the hour that you will see new philanthropists coming forth out of the community. These new phi-lanthropists will literally save communities from oppression and rescue a people from the ignorance in which they have lived."

Black Colleges of America

"This is the hour that you will see a great turn around in the black colleges of America. This is the hour that you will see great and large donations being given to them out of their own community. This is the hour that you will come face to face with major conditions concerning housing and commu-nity development. This is the season that things will not be as they were before," saith the Lord.

"I will make you wise concerning situations and conditions in Africa at this time. This is the day of great clarity in which you will make many choices as a people. You shall start mak-ing global money and have many lucrative opportunities. In 1999, you will start to see massive changes in South Africa again as the world starts to move towards the year 2000."

"You will see great men and women leave out of the commu-nity to move on to the next life, and they shall leave behind a legacy for another generation to take hold of and move their people into their next season," saith the Lord.

The Enslavement

I heard a roaring in the earth, and I heard the sound of con-troversy and the approach of a period of upset. And the Lord said, "This will be the time that wealth will start to generate among those that have tasted the bitter quinine of slavery in this nation. You will start to see a people coming into their own, and a new immigrant will sit in the seat of oppression in a system."

"The laws will rapidly change concerning immigration, and you will start to see laws put on the books that will bring a people to this country thinking it will be a land of opportunity, but in reality, it will be another kind of slavery," saith the Lord. "You will see entire villages raised up for this community, and they will not be allowed to visit certain parts of your cities."

The Weather Shall Prophesy

"Know that I will make you rest in My Presence," saith the Lord. "I will cause you to discover the hidden messages of this day. I will make the weather conditions change so rapidly that you will not be able to discern one season from the next."

"This will be the hour that you will see winters come with temperatures that shall literally feel like spring. This will be the time that you will witness the beginning of the earth warming itself. I will cause you to make a new headway in life. This is the time for you to see great conditions on every level. I will make you to understand the plan and arrangements that will lift you to a new place in authority," saith the Lord.

The Nations Shall Rebel

"This is the hour that you will start to see nations climb to the forefront, voicing their statements and declaring that they refuse to be policed by foreign nations."

"I now come to settle the score with you," saith the Lord. "I will cause an insurrection of small nations to move this country to a place of giving them their freedom, and out of this, I will make them to be nations that will survive on their own.

"The hour does come that you must now have people that will come forth with great intellect, and you will see society change as a whole. This will make you listen to wisdom on many levels. I will cause you to see discoveries come out of these small nations that will bring them into their own wealth and economic empowerment."

"I now bring you into a new climate, and you will see things radically changed. A New Order will begin to come forth, and many shall wonder at My doings," saith the Lord.

Written Judgments 4

Chapter 6
Special Visitation

In this chapter...

Reservoirs Contaminated 67
Days of Assassinations 68
The Caribbean Currency 69
Africa... The New Asia. 70
Bomb Scares 70
Wall Street 71
False Stock Markets 71
Class Racism 72
Concentration Camps / Training Camps. . . 72
Green Cards. 73
Changes in the Papacy 75
Trinidad, Jamaica, and Guyana 76
Bankrupting Social Security. 77
Cuba Comes Out 78

I hear the Word of the Lord saying, "This is the time and season in which I will cause special visitation to come upon the earth. I will make you see the wisdom of the ages. This is the season that I will cause new elevation to come to those that will worship Me in Spirit and in Truth."

"The Day of the Lord is upon you that you will experience the handiwork of God. This is the hour that you will see great tremors hit the northeast of America that will leave scientists baffled about the conditions of the day."

Reservoirs Contaminated

"The days of transformation will be upon you in such a way that you will see the reservoirs contaminated. It will be the days that the waters will become tainted with a chemical that will become detrimental to all that drink of it. I will make you to know the time and season that you are standing within this hour," saith the Lord.

"Make way! Make way! For this is the time that I will release great days of communication upon the earth. The way man communicated in the past will not be the way of communication and transportation in the future. The hour is upon you that you will see workstations in all kinds of areas and intelligence will increase on every level in this country."

"The days will come upon you that you will literally see a new platform of government come to the land. The system that is known as "voting" will be totally reworked in this hour. I will raise you up as a witness to the hour of the old orders, and men shall contrive ways to dissolve them."

"I come upon the earth in an unusual way. This is the time that you will see a visitation upon the sea world. The hour will come that you will not be able to eat the creatures of the seas. This will be the time that you will see judgement come to the society, and many jobs will be lost."

"The hour is upon you that you will see an awakening, and the days will be upon you that you shall come to the knowledge of My will and purpose. I make open your eyes to a season that will be the opening of a new chapter in the earth, " saith the Lord.

Days of Assassinations

"Come and behold the days of greater visitations! I will cause you to witness the days of assassinations. There will be the ending of many lives called to make important decisions that will change the world. It shall be a day of mourning and a day of rejoicing. I will make you wise in this hour to see the individuals that shall make the earth come to a standstill." "This is the time that you will see new laws coming to the table. I will cause you to develop in many areas in this hour. This is the time that you will see with greater clarity, and the hour of laughter shall be upon you."

The Caribbean Currency

'The tide is turning in the Caribbean. You're going to see the merging of the islands of the sea come together under one government and under one economy and under one dollar that's going to change the entire currency. They will be forced to grasp and merge together as one for the purpose of survival to open free trade for the world. Some leaders are going to die in the process because they're lining their pockets, and others are going to be suddenly moved off the scene."

"You are now coming into the days of the emergence of independent parties in this nation and within nations abroad. You're going to see new authorities coming into the forefront. It will appear as a rebellious order at first glance, but it will be divine order because it will be the order that is designed for the turn of the century. You're going to see entire nations almost wiped out over issues of debate, and others that will refuse to embrace change. I will cause other islands to be evacuated, only to bring a new people to settle on that land."

"You will also begin to see a great turnaround where individuals that are conservative will become liberals, and liberals will become conservative. There is going to be great mayhem in the nations of the world, and people will not know which way the wind is blowing. This will also be the hour that you're going to see major corporations that have been leading in the field of economics literally fold up overnight. It will be quicker than overnight — one hour they will be standing, and the next hour you will hear that their doors are shut and everything will be liquidated."

"You are coming into the days where new families are getting ready to grasp for the jewel of the wealth of this nation. You have seen the days of the Rockefellers and the Fords, and you have heard of the Vanderbilts; you've seen different high societies, but even that is changing. There is going to be new money and new economics that are getting ready to come forth without the permission of those that have held the ruling jewels in this land."

Africa... The New Asia
The Word of the Lord also comes to me saying, "Get ready! Watch out! For even Africa is going to take on such a change that it will literally become the new Asia of today. I am going to cause such shaking and rumbling in governments that you're going to begin to see nations that have been divided come into oneness and unity."

"There's getting ready to be a redirecting of not only commerce, but there is going to be a change in the currents at sea. I shall touch the way the waters carry the tide. The waters shall literally turn against certain nations, and they are not going to be able to export the way they used to."

Bomb Scares
"I'm going to redirect transportation in the airwaves and at sea. For what used to be major borders shall become weak borders, for I am getting ready to change the borders and how one goes in and out of the nations of the world. Even through

this, you'll begin to see a great multiplication of bomb scares. You will begin to see the great uprising of groups in the nation that shall literally start a war within this government. You will begin to see the coming forth of extreme groups that will begin to move into the forefront, and their voices will be heard. And there shall be great shaking and rumblings of governments."

"The election process as you have known it in America shall not exist much longer. They're going to give you something that will satisfy you, but the entire process is going to be revamped," says the Lord.

Wall Street

"I am getting ready to show you great signs, and you're going to see a great increase in the economy from this point to the end of the year, going into the New Year. The stock market is going to hit an all time high, and be jumping and bouncing with great optimism. But watch the bounce, because 24 months after that, there shall be a sudden drop and men in extreme agony will be standing on rooftops to dive headfirst to the concrete below."

"You will literally begin to see, before the turn of the century, individuals lose entire fortunes. But there is coming a jubilee on Wall Street, and I'm going to cause things that are not of Me to crumble in the blink of an eye."

False Stock Markets

"Arabs and Japanese will begin to create a false stock market that will begin to funnel in a lot of money to feed the greed in America, and they shall begin to suddenly pull a blanket out, for the war of Hiroshima is not over," saith God. "The war is yet continuing in the hearts and minds of those that will never forget their loss. You shall see your banks clamoring together overnight to merge with even greater merges that you saw in the eighties."

'The days are going to come when you are also going to hear of Congressmen who have huge accounts in other nations. Secret alliances are getting ready to be exposed and brought to the forefront in greater degrees than you can even imagine."

Class Racism
"There shall be a great shaking, even in Washington. It shall be a greater shaking than the nation has ever known. The next election is going to be a polarization of the nation."

"You are getting ready to see the days where people are going to set new standards of values, and racism as you have known it shall not be the racism of today, for there is a new racism coming and it is class racism," saith the Lord.

Concentration Camps...Training Camps
"You will see the entire education department revamped in the nation. You will see the homeless dilemma beginning to be managed and reconstructed. You will now step into the days where you are going to see concentration camps in manifestation, but they won't be called "concentration camps." Hear these words: they will be called "training camps." Hidden behind their mask of nobility will be the slow elimination of the undesirables of the day. I will give you a sign. I'll open up your eyes to begin to see this," saith the Lord.

"Around the month of November, there's going to be something like a sudden death; something that's going to cause a real tremor. It will be like the earth is shaking under your feet. Get ready, because even creation is in groaning and travailing to prepare for a day for which you shall now be ready."

Get ready, because you are going to find keys in the street for any kind of property that you desire. There is going to be a national plan that is going to go into effect to move Americans into home ownership so that they can begin to take control of their destiny."

"The government is getting ready to change the way it does business, and you're going to see a lot of things transferred on the local level," saith God, "and you're going to see things changing rapidly...rapidly...rapidly!"

Green Cards
"The immigration laws shall also be changed, for I am going to open up a window of opportunity. There shall be a flood of green cards that are going to be given if you're in the right place at the right time. And then the window will shut--never to be opened again."

"I am re-shaping and re-designing your lives. There will be a new group of preachers, ministers and those who will come forth to carry the gospel."

"You're going to move into the age of signs and wonders. The days are going to come when there will be signs, wonders, and phenomenal things manifesting in your midst, and you won't have a single scientific law in your realm that will explain what I'm doing. You're going to come into a moment where I'm going to perform signs through your children, and you'll be amazed at the knowledge that they will perceive and that which they will know."

"You are now coming into the days where life shall be extended. It will be nothing to meet someone who is 100 or 120. There shall be a sign in the earth that I shall give you of one that shall come who shall be close to 150. There's going to be signs and miraculous breakthroughs in the area of health and science."

"Now," the Lord would say, "brace yourself, for there is another upset that is coming in the fast food industry. You will begin to hear of deaths that will take place behind the way beef is processed. I've already given you the signs, but this will be as if it will wipe out an entire village. Even when this sign begins to come, it is going to affect the entire trucking industry. Meat will be thrown overboard and burned, and there will be a plan to try to handle it in secret. Even this is already exposed, but they're just trying to sweep it under the carpet. But the problem is getting ready to accelerate because the virus is connected with another virus and there's a new strain of infection."

This will be the sign: You shall begin to hear them begin to say, "You must move this beef off of the shelf after so many days." This will be the sign you are to eliminate that out of your diet for a season."

"You're going to see so many things that are getting ready to come up, and you will say, "Yes, I know that," "Yes, I know that," "Yes, the Lord has already spoken that unto us." Things that will be alarming to the world shall only be rejoicing unto those that know My Voice, for then you'll know that I am in the midst of thee. While others are stunned in amazement and frozen to the TV screen, you'll go around tending to your daily business because you'll say, "I know that God has spoken through His prophet."

Changes in the Papacy

"The papacy is going to change. There's going to be a change in the Pope. This one is moving on, and there is a new one coming to sit in the seat of authority. This one will be stern and firm, yet liberal, and he will move the Catholic Church to a new level of influence."

"You are going to also see the raising up, revamping and a new breath of wind that is going to go into dead places, and I now blow in the Catholic Church," saith God.

"You shall begin to see a change in the seat of authority, even in New York. There shall be something that will be tossed up, even in the next 20 to 23 months; something that's going to be up for grabs. But," the Lord says, "this will fall in the hands of right individuals."

"Get ready, because I am going to work a miracle in situations of child care and health care for those that will give themselves to children, for My law is going into effect, "Suffer little children to come unto Me and forbid them not." There shall be special blessings that shall come to those who minister to children. There's going to be a flood of new resources and new preparations."

Now the Lord would say, "I give unto you peace to do business, peace to negotiate, peace to handle business, peace to discern your wealth, peace to begin to move about and to care for things that you've been believing Me to move in."

There's a new order of prophets that shall come in the land. There are new voices that shall come to the forefront in the Church. Now watch this," saith God; "starting in the month of February of '98, there shall be leaders that are going on to be with the Lord. They're going to move on. They're going to be handing batons to the next generation. The relay race is almost over and they're handing their baton to others. You've heard in times past of "the changing of the guards." Now, you're going to see the removal of the guards."

Trinidad, Jamaica, Guyana
"There shall be great changes in governments such as Trinidad, Jamaica and Guyana; great changes and startling turnarounds. There shall be youth that shall occupy seats of influence. It's going to be like a sudden uprising in universities and on campuses. You're going to see great days of turning, where the clock is going to be turned back in time only to get back the gains of what has been lost and robbed."

"There's going to be a re-shaping in Haiti in this hour, and it will happen in a place that has seen and witnessed great devastation. The law has been fulfilled, and there's a new mind occupying seats of government that's about to bring the people out of bondage and captivity, for the sea shall begin to give up its dead. What has been robbed in the sea shall now be returned and multiplied, for that law is now fulfilled."

"Much of that which I will begin to declare unto you shall even be like a parable. But in the day of its fulfillment, you'll begin to look up and say, "Yea God, Yea God, Yea God. Oh God, that meaneth that, and this meaneth this, and that meaneth that; but what meaneth this?"

"I'll begin to show you signs in the heavens. There is something appearing in your galaxy that shall baffle the minds of the world. There will be something that will fall out of the heavens that will cause vast news coverage; "Was that a satellite or was that a piece of a planet or what?" "Will it burn up before it hits our atmosphere or what?" It shall be a mystery, and out of that there shall be another sudden appearance. There are planets in your galaxy, and more are getting ready to appear. This is why life will be extended; the years will literally be longer."

Bankrupting Social Security
"I'm bankrupting Social Security. This generation will eat up all the money. Life is coming upon you in such a way that you're going to hear coverage about the age process reversing. It shall be like a miracle that hit the earth. Some states will initiate mercy killing, because some just won't die. There will be some crying out for death, and death will flee from them. I'm appearing in your atmosphere. There will be families that will fight and say, "I'll stick him with the needle; give me the needle." You'll hear of people that won't die that should be dead because there's a sign that is coming in the earth."

"You are suspended in a moment of time at this very moment. Even now, you're caught up in a realm, your children are caught up in a realm, and even the babies are caught up in a realm. Even now they understand more than you do. I give you a sign."

"What is not together shall begin to correct itself because you're caught up in a moment of time. If you'll listen within yourself, I will show you how to correct yourself because you're caught up in a moment of time."

"I'm giving you even signs that shall appear in the next 3 days. You're going to see some things that are getting ready to come out on the local level which is going to make you stand back and say, "What in God's Name is going on?" It will be a period of great disgust."

Cuba Comes Out

"I change your direction. Get ready, for Cuba is coming out. Cuba shall become the new vacation resort, and place of travel. Cuba will bankrupt some of the major islands of the sea. There shall be fruit and vegetables that will come out of Cuba, and you wouldn't even want to taste other oranges or fruit from other places. I've done a miracle in their soil and kept a land from pollution, as you have known. I'm going to give you a sign out of Cuba because the leadership is about to take a new turn. That cycle is now over," saith the Lord.

"You shall see reconnection with loved ones. You shall see people going back and forth across the border. You're going to see a new income, and a new economy. This will come upon your shores. And when this hits," saith God, "get ready, because it means revival is going to sweep in Spanish-speaking nations."

"Now," the Lord says, "Get ready, because there's an abundance of rain that's coming; an abundance of natural rain to dry places. There's going to be so much rain that this nation will not know drought for a long time. There are some changes in temperatures, climate and atmosphere. I will give you a sign; the days will come where you will see a rose bloom in the winter."

"In the window of this moment, begin lifting up your hands and tell Me what you want. I'll tell you how to get it. You shall hear the still small Voice from within to show you the route and the path, and you shall exercise a new strength and dominion, for you've stepped into a new day," saith the Lord.

ZOE
MINISTRIES

P.O. Box 270 • New York, NY 10008
Call (212) 316-2177
To Order by Phone

Name_____

Address_____

City _____ State ____ Zip Code _____

Day Phone _____ Evening Phone _____

Grand Total $_____.___ Check __ Money Order __ Cash __ Credit Card __

Credit Card # _____ Exp. Date _____

Signature _____

BOOKSTORES:
Call for
Volume
Discounts!

QTY	TITLE	EACH	TOTAL
	Mentoring: The Missing Link	$10	
	Mentoring: The Iconoclastic Approach to Development of Ministry	$10	
	The Mastery of Mentorship	$10	
	Servanthood	$10	
	Spiritual Protocol	$20	
	The Spirit of the Oppressor	$10	
	The Spirit of Liberation	$10	
	His Color Was Black: A Race Attack	$10	
	Keys to Liberation	$10	
	The Power of the Dime	$10	
	The Power of Money	$10	
	The Achiever's Guide to Success	$10	
	Praise and Worship	$20	
	Breaking Soul Ties and Generational Curses	$10	
	Meditation: Key to New Horizons in God	$10	
	The Holy Spirit	$10	
	Prayer and Fasting	$10	
	The Joshua Generation	$10	
	The Making of the Dream	$10	
	Written Judgments Volume 1	$10	
	Written Judgments Volume 2	$10	
	Written Judgments Volume 3	$10	
	Written Judgments Volume 4 - **NEW RELEASE** -	$10	
	The Seed of Destiny	$10	
	Prophetic Genesis	$10	
	The Science of Prophecy	$10	
	School of the Prophets Volume 1	$50	
	School of the Prophets Volume 2	$50	
	The Science of Prophetic Leadership	$10	
	What Every Woman Should Know About Men	$10	
	Above All Things Get Wisdom	$1	
	Calling Forth the Men of Valor	$1	
	The Purpose of Tongues	$1	
	Keys to Your Success	$1	